PENGUIN CLASSICS

THE DHAMMAPADA

ADVISORY EDITOR: BETTY RADICE

The Dhammapada is a collection of 423 aphorisms which, in Pali verse form, are revered by southern Buddhists as illustrative of the Buddhist *dhamma* or moral system. It was incorporated before the beginning of the Christian era into the fifth section (*nikàya*) of the Pali *sutta-pitaka*, or collection of sermons.

JUAN MASCARÓ was born in Majorca. The beauty of the island, then unspoilt, and the strength of the living folk tradition made a deep impression on him as a child. At the age of thirteen he copied a book on occultism, but this proved spiritually misleading. However, a reading of the *Bhagavad Gita* he found highly illuminating, although it was in a poor translation, and this led him to learn the elements of Sanskrit. Later he went to Cambridge, where he read modern and oriental languages, Sanskrit, Pali and English.

He lectured in Oxford, on the Spanish mystics, and then went to Ceylon, where he was Vice-Principal of Parameshvara College at Jaffna, and to the University of Barcelona, where he was Professor of English. After the Spanish Civil War he settled permanently in England. He lived at first on the hills above Tintern Abbey; he translated some *Upanishads* and began the translation of the *Bhagavad Gita*, both Penguin Classics. He then returned to Cambridge University where he was a supervisor in English and lectured on 'Literary and Spiritual Values in the Authorized Version of the Bible'. He married Miss Kathleen Ellis in 1951 and they had a son and daughter. Juan Mascaró died in 1987. *The Times* obituary described him as a man who had 'achieved the unique feat of translation from languages not his own (Sanskrit and Pali) into another language not at first his own (English). His aim – decried by some academic critics but appreciated by thousands of readers all over the world – was to convey the essence of the original in pure, poetic English . . . His translations of the *Gita*, *Upanishads* and *Dhammapada* are the best that we have in English, and are unlikely to be superseded.'

THE
DHAMMAPADA

THE PATH OF PERFECTION

—

TRANSLATED FROM THE PALI
WITH AN INTRODUCTION BY
JUAN MASCARÓ

PENGUIN BOOKS

PENGUIN BOOKS

Published by the Penguin Group
Penguin Books Ltd, 80 Strand, London WC2R 0RL, England
Penguin Putnam Inc., 375 Hudson Street, New York, New York 10014, USA
Penguin Books Australia Ltd, 250 Camberwell Road, Camberwell, Victoria 3124, Australia
Penguin Books Canada Ltd, 10 Alcorn Avenue, Toronto, Ontario, Canada M4V 3B2
Penguin Books India (P) Ltd, 11 Community Centre, Panchsheel Park, New Delhi – 110 017, India
Penguin Books (NZ) Ltd, Cnr Rosedale and Airborne Roads, Albany, Auckland, New Zealand
Penguin Books (South Africa) (Pty) Ltd, 24 Sturdee Avenue, Rosebank 2196, South Africa

Penguin Books Ltd, Registered Offices: 80 Strand, London WC2R 0RL, England

www.penguin.com

This translation published 1973

055

Printed and bound in Great Britain by Clays Ltd, Elcograf S.p.A.

Set in Monotype Perpetua

ISBN-13: 978-0-14-044284-7

www.greenpenguin.co.uk

CONTENTS

CONTENTS

THE DHAMMAPADA

ACKNOWLEDGEMENTS

I wish to tender grateful acknowledgements to the following for permission to quote copyright passages in my Introduction:

The University Press, Cambridge, for a quotation from *Jalal 'Ud-Din Rumi* translated by Prof. R. A. Nicholson; and the Trustees of Rabindranath Tagore and Macmillan & Co. Ltd, London, for the quotation of a poem from *Gitanjali*.

J.M.

INTRODUCTION

T H E Pali word *Dhamma* corresponds to the Sanskrit *Dharma*, the first word of the *Bhagavad Gita* when the field of *Dharma*, the field of Truth, is mentioned. Pali, the language of the Buddhist scriptures of Ceylon, Burma and Indochina, is connected with Sanskrit just as Italian is connected with Latin. As in Italian, most words end in a vowel sound, and most consonants are softened to a double consonant: thus Sanskrit *Dharma* becomes *Dhamma* in Pali, and *Nirvana* becomes *Nibbana*. The Pali scriptures are reckoned to be about eleven times as long as the Bible. Besides the scriptures in Pali, there is a vast Buddhist literature written in Sanskrit and in Chinese and Tibetan translations.

The word *Dhamma* is of supreme importance in Buddhism, and behind the mere word there is the highest spiritual meaning. *Dhamma* comes from the Sanskrit root DHR, which carries the meaning 'to support, to remain' and thus of 'law, a moral law, a spiritual law of righteousness, the eternal law of the Universe, Truth'. In Christian terms it corresponds to 'the will of God'. *Pada*, both in Sanskrit and Pali, means 'foot, step' and thence has the meaning of a path. Thus *Dhammapada* suggests the Path of *Dhamma*, the right path of life which we make with our own footsteps, our own actions, and which leads us to the supreme Truth. The *Dhammapada* is the path of Truth, the path of light, the path of love, the path of life, the path of Nirvana. In Christian terms it is the path of God. Even if we do not reach the end of the path, the joys of the pilgrimage are ours. We can buy them 'without money and without price'. What is in truth the Path supreme becomes for us all the Path of Perfection.

The word Buddha comes from the root BUDH, to be awake, to be conscious of, to know. From the same root comes the

9

word *Buddhi* found in the *Bhagavad Gita* and meaning in different contexts: intelligence, reason, vision, wisdom. It is the faculty of man that helps him to distinguish what is good and beautiful from what is evil and ugly, what is true from what is false, and thus helps him to walk on the path where the great prayer of the Upanishads finds its fulfilment:

> From delusion lead me to Truth.
> From darkness lead me to Light.
> From death lead me to Immortality.

The progress of man on this earth is a slow awakening, and every poetical or artistic vision and every discovery is an awakening; but behind man's visions of something infinite in the finite and of something eternal in things that pass away that make possible his creations of art and poetry and all the discoveries of science, there is the great awakening into the law of Dharma, the eternal Nirvana, the Kingdom of heaven.

The call for an awakening is heard from many spiritual seers. We hear Kabir, 1440–1518, the Indian saint and poet, saying:

O friend, awake, and sleep no more! The night is over and gone, would you lose your day also? You have slept for unnumbered ages; this morning will you not awake?

Tr. Rabindranath Tagore

We can listen to the great poetry of Jalal'ud-Din Rumi, 1207–1273, the Sufi mystic in his Shamsi Tabriz:

O lovers, O lovers, it is time to abandon the world;
The drum of departure reaches my spiritual ear from heaven.
Behold, the driver has risen and made ready the file of camels,
And begged us to acquit him of blame: why, O travellers, are you asleep?
These sounds before and behind are the din of departure and of the camel-bells;

With each moment a soul and a spirit is setting off into the
Void.
From these stars like inverted candles, from these blue awnings
of the sky
There has come forth a wondrous people, that the mysteries may
be revealed.
A heavy slumber fell upon thee from the circling spheres:
Alas for this life so light, beware of this slumber so heavy!
O soul, seek the Beloved, o friend, seek the Friend,
O watchman, be wakeful: it behoves not a watchman to sleep.
On every side is clamour and tumult, in every street are torches
and candles,
For tonight the teeming world gives birth to the world ever-
lasting.
Thou wert dust and art a spirit, thou wert ignorant and art
wise.

Tr. R. A. Nicholson

Buddha was the name given to the Indian prince Gotama,
563-483 B.C., when after six years of strenuous spiritual
struggle he awoke into the infinite Light. In the radiance of
this Light he gave us words of wisdom and love, words that
have helped travellers in times past, that help us now, and
that shall help men in times to come. Because whatever an
unimaginable future may bring to man in ages unborn, the
great words of his spiritual leaders shall be for ever his Light;
and the words of Jesus give expression to this truth: 'Heaven
and earth shall pass away, but my words shall not pass away'.
What has been a Light for a few shall be in time a Light for
all.

Buddha was a prince and was born to be a king, but he
felt the vanity of earthly kingdoms and longed for a kingdom of heaven, Nirvana.

In the poetical story of Buddha's childhood and youth we
are told that his father, the king, in fear that his only son
might one day leave his court and become a mendicant
ascetic, as it was foretold at his birth, decided to surround
the prince with all kinds of pleasures, built for him three

palaces for the three Indian seasons and arranged that his son might never see an old man, a sick man, a corpse, or a mendicant ascetic. As fate decreed, the young prince in time saw the four, and the mystery of the sorrow of life did not allow him to rest. He felt the longing for something real behind the transience of things, that longing that made the Hebrew prophet say:

> As the hart panteth after the water brooks,
> So panteth my soul after thee, O God.
> My soul is athirst for God, for the living God:
> When shall I come and appear before God?,

Or as the old English song:

> Hierusalem, my happy home,
>   When shall I come to thee?
> When shall my sorrows have to end,
>   Thy joys when shall I see?

Or as the Castilian poet Jorge Manrique, 1440–79, begins his magnificent poem: 'Let our sleeping soul remember, and be awake and be alive, in contemplation, of how our life passes away, of how our death comes forward to us, so silently'.

It is the sorrow which impels Shelley to sing:

> We look before and after,
>   And pine for what is not:
> Our sincerest laughter
>   With some pain is fraught;
> Our sweetest songs are those that tell of saddest thought.

It is the feeling that there is a division in us, a separation from something infinite with which we want to be reunited, because we are like a lost little child who is crying in the dark for his home.

The young prince did not know, but he was longing: he was not happy in the established conventions of his time. He felt that in order to find something higher he had to cut a path through the jungle of desires and fears, of illusions and contradictions. He knew that power and pleasures only mean a little life and a little death. His 'arrows of desire' impelled him, in the words of the *Upanishad*, to travel from darkness to Light, from the unreal to the Real, from death to Immortality. He must leave the palace and his lovely wife and baby son. He must first find salvation and then return for the salvation of all men, for the salvation of those he left in the palace. How touching is the description of the departure of the future Buddha from his wife and his baby son Rahula :

Now the future Buddha, after he had sent Channa on his errand, thought to himself, 'I will just take one look at my son'; and, rising from the couch on which he was sitting, he went to the suite of apartments occupied by the mother of Rahula, and opened the door of her chamber. Within the chamber was burning a lamp fed with sweet-smelling oil, and the mother of Rahula lay sleeping on a couch strewn deep with jasmine and other flowers, her hand resting on the head of her son. When the future Buddha reached the threshold, he paused, and gazed at the two forms where he stood.

'If I were to raise my wife's hand from off the child's head, and take him up, she would awake, and thus prevent my departure. I will first become a Buddha, and then return and see my son.' So saying, he descended from the palace.

Tr. H. C. Warren

Prince Gotama leaves his palace by night and goes into the Unknown. That night seems a symbol of a verse in the *Bhagavad Gita*.

In the dark night of all beings awakes to Light the tranquil man. But what is day to other beings is night for the sage who sees. 2.69

It is the night of Saint John of the Cross, 1542-91, when in one of the most sublime poems of all literature he tells us that the soul 'aflame with longings of love' leaves her home in deep darkness, in a night of silence, and goes for her great adventure 'with no light nor guide, except the Light that was burning in my heart'.

> Sin otra luz y guía,
> Sino la que en el corazón ardía.

Buddha left for the great adventure of all men who long for life and 'having put his hand to the plough' he never looked back. His spiritual struggle lasted for six long years until at last, in despair, he sat under the Bodhi tree with the heroic determination either to die or to find eternal life. His heroism had its reward. During that night Buddha saw the Wheel of becoming, the Four great truths, the Path of eight perfections, the Middle Way and at last NIRVANA, Truth.

What is the Truth that Buddha tells us he found? Other spiritual leaders say they found Truth. Reason tells us that Truth must be One. We know that science is perpetual progress, but that the spirit of science which leads the scientific world into their great adventure is one. We know that there are great poems composed in languages past and present, that those poems are poetry, but that the spirit of poetry is one. We know there are many sacred books and that there are different religions, but if we read the sacred books carefully and spiritually, we see that the highest in them, their most spiritual and moral elements, is one. And we know that in spite of many countries and races there is something in the spirit of man which a sensitive person feels as one. The Truth of the universe must be One, even as the spirit of science, of poetry, and of religion and humanity is one. Is it the One which Buddha found and the greatest spiritual leaders have found? 'Seek and ye shall find.'

Science walks on the earth. Poetry flies above the earth. Both are necessary for the progress of man; but his progress is his pilgrimage and his pilgrimage is his becoming. Beyond becoming there is Being, and from Being comes love and comes the good and the beautiful; but neither love, nor the good, nor the beautiful can be seen by the telescope or the microscope. This is why the poetry of the past is never old as the science of the past is.

Buddha found NIRVANA, the union of the finite with the Infinite, that Truth that according to the *Kena Upanishad*, 'comes to the thought of those who know him beyond thought, not to those who think it can be attained by thought'. It is the *Nirvana* mentioned in the *Bhagavad Gita* when it says:

The Yogi who, lord of his mind, ever prays in this harmony of soul, attains the peace of Nirvana, the peace supreme that is in me. 6.15

And also in the last verse of the second chapter:

This is the Eternal in man, O Arjuna. Reaching him, all delusion is gone. Even in the last hour of his life upon earth, man can reach the Nirvana of Brahman – man can have peace in the peace of his God.

Tradition tells that when Buddha found Nirvana under the Bodhi tree, he poured out his joy of liberation in the two famous verses of the *Dhammapada*:

I have gone round in vain the cycles of many lives ever striving to find the builder of the house of life and death. How great is the sorrow of life that must die!

But now I have seen thee, housebuilder: never more shalt thou build this house. The rafters of sins are broken, the ridge-pole of ignorance is destroyed. The fever of craving is past: for my mortal mind is gone to the joy of the immortal NIRVANA. 153, 154

The description of NIRVANA given by Buddha in Udana 8 can be compared to that of the fourth state of consciousness of the *Mandukya Upanishad* and with the four stages of prayer of Saint Teresa:

A condition there is, brethren, wherein earth, water, fire and air are not; wherein is neither consciousness, nor space, nor a void. Neither this world nor a world beyond are there, neither are there the sun and the moon. It is not a coming, it is not a going, nor a standing still, nor a falling, nor a rising.

That is the end of sorrow. That is Nirvana.

There is also, brethren, that which is not born, nor become, nor made. If that were not, there would be no refuge from that which is born, is become, is made.

That is the end of sorrow. That is Nirvana.

Saint Teresa, 1515–82, describes in Christian terms four ways of prayer which can be compared to what the *Yoga Sutras* tell us, or to the Buddhist meditations. She speaks of our making a garden where we plant the seeds of our good works in life. That garden must be watered by the waters of love. Those waters we can draw in four ways: out of a well with buckets, a laborious way; by using the wheel of a windlass, a machine for drawing water; by the waters of a stream; or by rain from heaven, the easiest way. The four ways correspond to recollection, meditation, contemplation and union.

Recollection requires attention and concentration. When it is pure, unselfish, unselfconscious, it goes beyond pleasure and it reaches joy, the joy of love.

The second stage is meditation: the mind thinks, but the thoughts are limited to a definite object. In this stage we find the use of thought in all forms. Most thought, including scientific, scholarly and philosophical thought belongs to that second stage. When thought is clear and used for something good and beautiful, we find the joy of meditation, and this joy is also love.

In the third stage there is contemplation, a much higher stage. St Teresa calls it 'prayer of quietness'. It is a silence of the mind. We are in the region of poetry and art, where there is greater joy and love. This cannot be reached by thought, because thought is sound not silence, and only silence in Eternity can go beyond sound in time. The knowledge that comes from contemplation is described in the *Bhagavad Gita*:

When one sees Eternity in things that pass away and Infinity in finite things, then one has pure knowledge. 18.20

Contemplation goes beyond thought and is a higher stage of joy and love. The silence of contemplation made possible such verses as those beginning the 'Ode on a Grecian Urn' of Keats:

> Thou still unravish'd bride of quietness,
> Thou foster-child of Silence and slow Time...

Thought alone can never create these verses of silent wonder, and thought alone can never understand them.

The fourth stage is called by St Teresa 'Prayer of Union'. This is beyond concentration or recollection, meditation and contemplation: it is the culmination of the highest man can reach. In that stage his becoming has stopped and he is pure Being. This is felt by Wordsworth when he says in his 'Lines Composed above Tintern Abbey':

> That serene and blessed mood,
> In which the affections gently lead us on, –
> Until, the breath of this corporeal frame
> And even the motion of our human blood
> Almost suspended, we are laid asleep
> In body, and become a living soul;
> While with an eye made quiet by the power
> Of harmony, and the deep power of joy,
> We see into the life of things.

It is in moments of Being when man has found THAT beyond words and thought and has called it Brahman, Atman, Elohim, God, Nirvana, Tao, Allah, or OM which according to the *Upanishads* includes all names, and other sacred words.

In a state of contemplation and union the knower and the known are one. Ego-consciousness has disappeared: the painter of the tree has become the tree. In the normal state of consciousness the mind is like a lamp that flickers in the winds of time, but in supreme oneness:

Then his soul is a lamp whose light is steady, for it burns in a shelter where no winds come. *Bhagavad Gita* 6.19

The great Japanese spiritual scholar Dr Daisetz T. Suzuki, 1871–1966, wrote two days before his death an Introduction to the book *A Flower Does not Talk* by Rev. Zenkei Shibayama, and what he says has a relevance in this connection:

Zen teaches us that in order to understand a mountain to be a mountain in the Zen way, the experience is to be negated first – a mountain is not a mountain – and it is only when this negation is understood that the affirmation 'a mountain is a mountain' becomes Reality.

The great task of man on earth is to see the Real behind the appearance of waking dreams, described by Shakespeare in *The Tempest*:

> Be cheerful, Sir.
> Our revels are now ended. These our actors,
> As I foretold you, were all spirits, and
> Are melted into air, into thin air:
> And, like the baseless fabric of this vision,
> The cloud-capp'd towers, the gorgeous palaces,
> The solemn temples, the great globe itself,
> Yea, all which it inherit, shall dissolve,
> And, like this insubstantial pageant faded,
> Leave not a rack behind. We are such stuff
> As dreams are made on; and our little life
> Is rounded with a sleep.

As to the joy felt in the high prayer of union, the *Chandogya Upanishad* says:

Where there is creation there is progress. Where there is no creation there is no progress: know the nature of creation.

Where there is joy there is creation. Where there is no joy there is no creation: know the nature of joy.

Where there is the Infinite there is joy. There is no joy in the finite.

Describing the stage of contemplation, 'The Prayer of Quietness', Saint Teresa says:

We begin to lose our craving for things of this earth; and no wonder, because one sees clearly that no riches, no power, no honours, no pleasures, can for a moment, even for the twinkling of an eye, give such true joy.

About the prayer of union she can only say what those who have attained a state beyond words can say:

Let us now speak of the joy felt when that union has been achieved. Let him who knows try to express it: it cannot be understood, how much less be put into words.

And according to the *Taittiriya Upanishad*:

Words and mind go to him, but reach him not and return. But he who knows the joy of Brahman, fears no more.

*

In union with Being the Upanishads found a condition that is 'neither outer nor inner consciousness, neither semi-consciousness nor unconsciousness', a condition that is 'peace and love'. Buddha found in NIRVANA a condition 'wherein there is neither consciousness, nor space nor a void. It is not a coming, it is not a going, nor a standing still, nor a falling, nor a rising'.

Saint John of the Cross, 1542–91, says that when the soul is in union she sees the splendour of God as many lamps of fire, his qualities: love, omnipotence, wisdom, mercy, justice, and many others. All these lamps of fire merge in the Lamp of the Being of God.

We thus see that at the end of the Path they all have found ONE who is in the many and to whom we all can go.

The good and the beautiful are the two great ideals of ancient Greece, the καλὸs καὶ ἀγαθόs. Plotinus, A.D. 205–270, expresses it in his philosophy:

To make our soul good and beautiful is to make ourselves like unto God: because God is beauty.

Ugliness is the same as evil: its contrary is beauty and good.

The love of the Beautiful, the true religion of Greece, was expressed by Keats in immortal words:

> Beauty is truth, truth beauty, – that is all
> Ye know on earth, and all ye need to know.

Keats had seen the Spirit of Beauty in all things and he knew that this Spirit is Truth: that was his supreme knowledge on earth, and that was all he needed to know. To see the beauty of nature and art is to see the truth of art and nature, and to see the beauty of the universe is to see the truth of the universe. When in his search for God Saint Augustine questions the heavens and the earth, he exclaims: 'My questioning with them was my thought, and their answer was their beauty.' It was the vision of the Hebrew poet:

> The heavens declare the glory of God,
> And the firmament sheweth his handiwork.

The true spiritual seer is a poet, whether he composes verse or not, and a radiance of beauty shines over his words: let us think of the beauty of the words of Jesus, and of his life as a life of beauty. Let us hear Buddha, the words of Buddha:

It is told that once Ananda, the beloved disciple of Buddha, saluted his master and said: 'Half the holy life, O master, is friendship with the beautiful, association with the beautiful, communion with the beautiful.'

'Say not so, Ananda, say not so!' the master replied. 'It is not half of the holy life. It is the whole of the holy life.'

*

'Some people,' said Buddha, the master, 'have accused me of uttering these words:

When one attains the release called the Beautiful, and abides therein, at such a time he considers the whole universe as ugly.

But I never said these words. This is what I do say:

When one attains the release called the Beautiful, at such a time he knows in truth what Beauty is'.

From the *Samyuta* and the *Digha Nikaya*

Love is beauty and beauty is truth, and this is why in the beauty of a flower we can see the truth of the universe. This is how Buddha speaks of love in the *Majjhima Nikaya*:

Buddha spoke thus once to his disciples: The words of men to you can be of five kinds: at the right time or at the wrong time, true or false, gentle or bitter, profitable or unprofitable, kindly or resentful.

If men speak evil of you, this must you think: 'Our heart shall not waver; and we will abide in compassion, in lovingkindness, without resentment. We will think of the man who speaks ill of us with thoughts of love, and in our thoughts of love shall we dwell. And from that abode of love we will fill the whole world with far-reaching, wide-spreading, boundless love'.

Moreover, if robbers should attack you and cut you in pieces with a two-handed saw, limb by limb, and one of you should feel hate, such a one is not a follower of my gospel.

*

The *Upanishads* are the path of light; the *Bhagavad Gita* is the path of love; the *Dhammapada* is the path of life. Buddha avoided metaphysical questions. He might have answered them in the words of Jesus: 'Seek ye first the kingdom of God and his righteousness; and all these things shall be added unto you'. Buddha therefore makes his teaching free from metaphysics. He simply says:

Do not what is evil. Do what is good. Keep your mind pure. This is the teaching of Buddha. *Dhammapada* 183

It is said that once a man of arms undertook a long journey to see a holy follower of Buddha, and asked if the message of Buddha could be taught to him. The answer was: 'Do not what is evil. Do what is good. Keep your mind pure. This is the teaching of Buddha'. 'Is this all?', said the man of arms; 'Every child of five knows this.' 'It may be so, but few men of eighty can practise it', he was told.

The first of the great truths of Buddha, that 'all is transient', and therefore all is sorrow, has been part of the vision of man through the ages expressed in the memorable words of Ecclesiastes: 'Vanity of vanities, saith the preacher, vanity of vanities; all is vanity'. But Buddha makes it very clear that it is only the transient life which is vanity, not the eternal life, or those moments of eternal life, which we can enjoy in our transitory life.

It is in the second of his great truths that Buddha makes his deep spiritual and psychological contribution to the problem of man: the cause that man suffers under the transient, under things that pass away, is that he clings to the transient, he craves for things that pass away, thus forgetting the ever-present Eternal in him. A few men in all times have longed for Eternity and have attained Eternity, but only a few. When the light seen by a few becomes the light of the many, then man will be able to fulfil himself on this earth. In the meanwhile we cannot but see the truth of the Song of God:

Among thousands of men perhaps one strives for perfection; and among thousands of those who strive perhaps one knows me in truth. *Bhagavad Gita* 7.3

Buddha makes craving the source of suffering and freedom from craving the source of liberation. As to the simple, necessary, earthly necessities the words of Jesus could be the words of Buddha: 'Seek ye first the kingdom.'

Of freedom from craving desires comes peace in man and between men. Freedom from desires is an undertone of

22

wisdom that runs through spiritual vision. The *Gita* makes it an absolute condition for liberation:

When a man surrenders all desires that come to his heart and by the grace of God finds the joy of God, then his soul has indeed found peace. 2.55

But the *Bhagavad Gita* also makes clear that there is an absolute difference between desire and a good will, and thus Krishna says:

I am the power of those who are strong, when this power is free from passions and selfish desires. I am desire when this is pure, when this desire is not against righteousness. 7.11

The great battle of the *Bhagavad Gita*, the battle of life, is the battle of contrary desires, and thus we hear: 'Be a warrior and kill desire, the powerful enemy of the soul'. 3.43

St John of the Cross says that all voluntary desires, great or small, or even the smallest, are in the way of union, because communion is the transformation of the will of man into the will of God, and the smallest selfish desire is a division, a separation.

In the *Samyuta Nikaya* we read this story:

Suffering, the cause of suffering, the end of suffering, and the Path that leads to the end of sufferings: these are the four truths of Buddha.

The son of Malunkya was old, and he was anxious to know the doctrine of Buddha in brief. He went to the Master who asked him:

Do you feel any craving, O son of Malunkya, for things which you never saw, which you do not see, and which you do not want to see in the future? – 'No, Master'.

Do you feel any craving for things which you never heard, which you do not hear, and which you do not want to hear? – 'No, Master'.

And the same could be asked about the other senses. Now, do you feel any craving for things you never thought, you do not think, and you do not want to think in the future? – 'No Master'.

Even as you have no craving for things that are not in your thoughts or senses, have no craving for things that are in your senses and in your thoughts. This is the path that leads to the end of suffering. – 'I have understood, Master.'

And the son of Malunkya saw the Truth, and left the Master with joy in his heart.

Rabindranath Tagore sings of the sorrow of man:

'Prisoner, tell me, who was it that bound you?'

'It was my master', said the prisoner. 'I thought I could outdo everybody in the world in wealth and power, and I amassed in my own treasure-house the money due to my king. When sleep overcame me I lay upon the bed that was for my lord, and on waking up I found I was a prisoner in my own treasure-house.'

'Prisoner, tell me who was it that wrought this unbreakable chain?'

'It was I,' said the prisoner, 'who forged this chain very carefully. I thought my invisible power would hold the world captive leaving me in freedom undisturbed. Thus night and day I worked at the chain with huge fires and cruel hard strokes. When at last the work was done and the links were complete and unbreakable, I found that it held me in its grip.'

The stopping of desires and the peace of liberation is suggested in the *Tao Te Ching*:

> Without going out of my door
> I can know all things on earth.
> Without looking out of my window
> I can know the ways of heaven.
>
> For the further one travels
> The less one knows.
>
> The sage therefore
> Arrives without travelling,
> Sees all without looking,
> Does all without doing. 47

The Middle Way of Buddha helps us to understand why there must be a peace from craving, from desires. This

Middle Way is the narrow path of perfection that leads to the top of the holy mountain as painted in some early editions of Saint John of the Cross. On the right there is the wrong path that leads to desire for things of the earth, and on the left the wrong path that leads to desire for things of heaven. Two verses of the *Bhagavad Gita* might refer to those two wrong paths:

There are men who have no vision, and yet they speak many words. They follow the letter of the Vedas, and they say: 'there is nothing but this'.

Their soul is warped with selfish desires, and their heaven is a selfish desire. They have prayers for pleasure and power, the reward of which is earthly rebirth. II. 42,43

But in the centre there is the narrow path that leads to the top of the mountain. That path suggests a harmony in life: 'not for him who eats too much, nor for him who eats too little; not for him who sleeps too little nor for him who sleeps too much', as the *Gita* says in 6.16. It is a Path of Perfection, as explained by Buddha in this story:

Sona Kolivisa was the son of a rich merchant who had joined the order of monks of Buddha. Through excess of zeal he had been walking on thorns and the path where he walked was covered with blood. Then he thought: 'And if I were to return to my home and use my wealth in doing good deeds?'

Buddha, the Master, knew his thoughts, and went to him and asked him:

'When you were at home, Sona, could you play the lute?' – 'Yes, Master.'

'When the strings of the lute were over-taut, did your lute give proper sounds?' – 'No, Master.'

'When the strings of your lute were neither over-taut nor over-slack the lute gave the proper sounds. Was it not so?' – 'It was so, Master.'

'Even so, Sona, an excess of zeal leads to self-exaltation, and a lack of zeal leads to indolence: have an evenness of zeal, master your powers in harmony. Be this your aim.'

And Sona Kolivisa heard the words of the Master and obeyed them; and in a short time reached Nirvana.

And what do we find at the top of the mountain of God? On the path we find the word *nada, nothing*, written five times: *nada, nada, nada, nada, nada*. And on the mountain is written, 'And on the mountain nothing', '*Y en el monte nada*'.

The path that leads to *nothing* is the path of the Infinite, mentioned in the *Tao Te Ching*: 'Go far into the Void and there rest in quietness'. It is the famous *Sunyata* of Buddhism. St John of the Cross wants to make clear the importance of nothing, in its positive and negative sense:

> That thou mayest have pleasure in everything,
> seek pleasure in nothing.
> That thou mayest know everything,
> seek to know nothing.
> That thou mayest possess all things,
> seek to possess nothing.
> That thou mayest be everything,
> seek to be nothing.

Father A. Baker, 1575–1641, explains in these words:

Nothing and nothing make nothing. Understand and bear in mind this mystic saying taken out of the practice of arithmetic, where one, being to add together two ciphers saith, as I said: 'Nothing and nothing make nothing'.

This is a state of perfect union, which is termed by some a state of nothing, and by others, with as much reason, a state of totality.

'But the Spirit is not this, is not this', says the *Brihad-Aranyaka Upanishad*.

Sunyata comes from a Sanskrit verbal root, SE, which has the negative meaning of *empty* and the positive meaning of *full*. The suggestion of emptiness is found in the *Dhammapada*: 'Empty the boat of your life', 369. And also when it says:

When with a mind in silent peace a monk enters his empty house, then he feels the unearthly joy of beholding the light of Truth. 373

It is clearly suggested in verse ninety-three :'

Who can trace the invisible path of the man who soars in the sky of liberation, the infinite Void without beginning?

When the Dhammapada was compiled, probably during the third century before Christ, a few ideas common to Indian thought may have been used, and original verses of the *Dhammapada* may in turn have found their way into Indian writings. If we select a few verses from the *Hitopadesa*, we may find the spirit of gentle irony and wisdom found in some verses of the *Dhammapada* :

Of what use are words of wisdom to the man who is unwise? Of what use is a lamp to a man who is blind?

Hear the essence of thousands of sacred books: to help others is virtue: to hurt others is sin.

A man rises or goes down by his own actions: like the builder of a wall, or as the digger of a well.

The narrow-minded man thinks and says: 'This man is one of us; this one is not, he is a stranger. To the man of noble soul the whole of mankind is but one family'.

But that the spirit of the *Dhammapada* is the spirit of Buddha is accepted both by his followers and by scholars.

Buddha wants us to stop the wheel of becoming so that we can rest in the centre of Being. He wants us to follow the middle Way which is the way of the *Bhagavad Gita*, and to be fully conscious of the four great truths and thus begin to follow the great Path. His message is a message of life, of life here and now, at this very moment, so that every moment of our life is a progress on the path of perfection. As to metaphysical questions he is silent, suggesting the metaphysical fact that the Supreme is beyond words. When asked whether a man lives after death, he might well have given the answer of one of his disciples:

We do not know whether he is the body, or in the body, or other than the body whilst alive: how can we know whether after the death of the body he is dead?

Buddha wants us to feel a sense of urgency in the solution of our spiritual problem, and use our reason for the solution of our moral problem. There is an old Indian prayer that could be a universal prayer for man:

May the evil man become good, and may the good man have peace. May he who has peace become free, and may he who is free make others free.

A verse of the *Dhammapada* expresses this sense of urgency:

How can there be laughter, how can there be pleasure, when the whole world is burning? When you are in deep darkness, will you not ask for a lamp? 146

The *Dhammapada* is a lamp. Let us think of the first two verses that tell us that if a man has a pure mind joy follows him, but that if he has an impure mind suffering follows him. The spirit of these verses is suggested in the *Maitri Upanishad*:

Samsara, the transmigration of life, takes place in one's mind. Let one therefore keep the mind pure, for what one thinks that he becomes: this is the mystery of Eternity.

The Sanskrit words beginning this sentence could be a motto for a book of psychology: *Cittam eva hi Samsaram*, the mind is *Samsara*. Every moment of our life is a new life and an old death: we die in a past that is gone and we live in a future to come, and thus our life on this earth is a perpetual transmigration.

*

The Path given by Buddha is a path of eight stages. The eight stages are eight perfections. From melodies and harmonies on the journey we arrive to the silence of Nirvana.

The *Maitri Upanishad* says:

The sound of Brahman is OM. At the end of OM there is silence. It is a silence of joy. It is the end of the journey where fear and sorrow are no more: steady, motionless, never-falling, ever-lasting, immortal.

In order to reach the Highest, consider in adoration the sound and silence of Brahman. For it has been said: 'God is sound and silence. His name is OM. Attain therefore contemplation – contemplation in silence on him'.

The first verses of the *Dhammapada* show us the beginning of the Path. In those verses a law of spiritual gravitation is given in sublime simplicity. A pure mind makes it possible to have right views, the first stage of the Path. A pure mind is like a clear mirror which reflects things but takes nothing, and sees them all under the same light. This pure mind is expressed in the words of Krishna: 'I am the same to all beings, and my love is ever one'. 9.29

It is suggested in the words of Jesus: 'If any man hear my words, and believe them not, I judge him not'. John 12.47

If we ask, what is right?, we may answer in the words of the *Dhammapada*:

The perfume of flowers goes not against the wind, not even the perfume of sandalwood of rose-bay or of jasmine; but the perfume of virtue travels against the wind and reaches unto the ends of the world. 54

In the first stage on the Path we also find the four virtues whose perfume 'reaches unto the ends of the world', the four great virtues of Buddhism, and indeed of all spiritual religion or humanism: *Maitri, Karuna, Mudita, Upeksha. Maitri, Metta* in Pali, is friendliness, good-will, benevolence, love, loving-kindness to all. *Karuna* is compassion, pity, sorrow for the sufferings of all. *Mudita* is joy in the good of all. *Upeksha* is forgiveness, overlooking the faults of all. These virtues help man to enter the Path and are his great friends on his journey.

'*Right views*' is a pure vision of the four great truths.

The second stage is *right determination*. We see the star over the Path of Perfection and we determine to follow the star, remembering the words of the *Upanishad*: 'A man comes with his actions to the end of his determination'. As the spiritual life is one, the words of Jesus can be quoted: 'No man, having put his hand to the plough, and looking back, is fit for the kingdom of God.'

The third stage is *right words*. The *Bhagavad Gita* says:

Words which give peace, words which are good and beautiful and true, and also the reading of sacred books: this is the harmony of words. 17.15

And the *Dhammapada* tells us: 'Better than a thousand useless words is one single word that gives peace'.

Buddha defines right words as 'words at the right time, true, profitable and kindly'. The ideal of truth is absolute. Only truth can save man.

The fourth stage is *right action*. It is the Karma Yoga of the *Bhagavad Gita*: good and pure work as an offering of love. This will fulfil the Indian verse of wisdom:

Hear the essence of thousands of sacred books: To help others is virtue; to hurt others is sin.

It will fulfil the sublime words of Jesus: 'Do good to them that hate you'.

The fifth stage is right means of supporting one's life, or *right livelihood*.

The man who follows the *Dhamma* of Buddha, or indeed the *Dhamma* of the great spiritual leaders, cannot earn his livelihood by working for the production and use of things that are useless, harmful or evil. Only an inner light and spiritual heroism can help man in his moral collective uplifting.

The sixth of the eight stages of the Path, of those perfections that like spiritual waves impel man to the shore of NIRVANA, is *right effort*.

Right effort means right tension and right relaxation. In concentration it means the right attention to something whilst there is a relaxing of everything not connected with the object of attention. All right effort is right in the sense that we never think it is an effort. Wise men of all times have seen this truth. Epictetus, A.D. 60–140, writes:

Know that there is nothing more easy to handle than the human soul. It needs but to will, and the thing is done: the soul is on the right path. On the contrary, it needs but to nod and all is lost. For ruin or recovery are from within.

We have to learn the paradox that to want not to think about something is in fact to be thinking about that something; and that as long as we think that it is an effort to discard undesirable thoughts or habits we make it an effort.

The seventh stage is *right remembrance*, a right mindfulness. It is an ever-remembering of the Path, a quiet watchfulness of life.

This is praised in the second chapter of the *Dhammapada* as 'the path of immortality' and suggested in chapter thirteen: 'Arise! Watch. Remember and forget not'.

Jesus says, 'Watch and pray'. St. John of the Cross speaks of 'silence and work'. In our darkness we remember the words of Isaiah:

Watchman, what of the night? Watchman, what of the night?

The watchman said, The morning cometh, and also the night: if ye will enquire, enquire ye: return, come. 21.11–12

The spiritual path is a watching, an enquiring and a returning.

The last of the eight waves of spiritual life that carry us to the other shore is called *Samadhi*, communion. It is the final communion of the finite with the Infinite, the end of the journey mentioned in the *Dhammapada*: 'The traveller has reached the end of the journey.' 90

The word SAM-A-DHI comes from the root DHA which means to hold in a place. With the prefix SAM and A, *Samadhi* suggests a union, a communion: the union with Brahman of the *Upanishads*, the union with God of the Christian mystics, the union with NIRVANA of Buddha.

The four stages of Samadhi mentioned in the Buddhist scriptures remind us of the four stages of prayer of St Teresa. The first stage of Samadhi is pure thought, recollection and meditation, and this is followed by the stopping of thought, contemplation. In those two stages there is a deep consciousness of joy and peace. In the third stage of the Buddhist Samadhi, the 'prayer of quietness' of St Teresa, the consciousness of joy which was common to the first two stages disappears; but there is still a consciousness of peace, a remnant of the consciousness of the 'I' in time. The burden of the ego at that stage is very light, but it is still with man; until in the final fourth stage NIRVANA is attained, the burden of the ego, the burden of life, has fallen for ever, and man is free:

The traveller has reached the end of the journey! In the freedom of the Infinite he is free from all sorrows, the fetters that bound him are thrown away, and the burning fever of life is no more.

Dhammapada 90

❋

The message of Buddha is in the *Dhammapada*, and the hearing of this message is joy:

Even as a lake that is pure and peaceful and deep so becomes the soul of the wiseman when he hears the words of DHAMMA.

Dhammapada 82

And the words of DHAMMA are words of Truth.

The message of Buddha is a message of joy. He found a treasure and he wants us to follow the path that leads to the treasure he found. He tells man that he is in deep darkness, but he also tells him that there is a path that leads to light. He wants us to arise from a life of dreams into a higher life where man loves and does not hate, where a man helps and does not hurt. His appeal is universal, because he appeals to reason and to the universal in us all: 'It is you who must make the effort. The Great of the past only show the way'. He achieves a supreme harmony of vision and wisdom by placing spiritual truth on the crucial test of experience; and only experience can satisfy the mind of modern man. He wants us to watch and be awake and he wants us to seek and to find.

In the *Dhammapada* we can hear the voice of Buddha. This gospel of light and of love is amongst the greatest spiritual works of man. Each verse is like a small star and the whole has the radiance of Eternity.

JUAN MASCARÓ

The Retreat,
Comberton, Cambridge
December 1971

1

CONTRARY WAYS

1 What we are today comes from our thoughts of yester-
day, and our present thoughts build our life of to-
morrow: our life is the creation of our mind.

   If a man speaks or acts with an impure mind, suffering follows him as the wheel of the cart follows the
beast that draws the cart.

2 What we are today comes from our thoughts of yester-
day, and our present thoughts build our life of to-
morrow: our life is the creation of our mind.

   If a man speaks or acts with a pure mind, joy follows
him as his own shadow.

3 'He insulted me, he hurt me, he defeated me, he robbed
me.' Those who think such thoughts will not be free
from hate.

4 'He insulted me, he hurt me, he defeated me, he robbed
me.' Those who think not such thoughts will be free
from hate.

5 For hate is not conquered by hate: hate is conquered
by love. This is a law eternal.

6 Many do not know that we are here in this world to live
in harmony. Those who know this do not fight against
each other.

7 He who lives only for pleasures, and whose soul is not
in harmony, who considers not the food he eats, is
idle and has not the power of virtue – such a man is
moved by MARA, is moved by selfish temptations, even
as a weak tree is shaken by the wind.

8 But he who lives not for pleasures, and whose soul is in self-harmony, who eats or fasts with moderation, and has faith and the power of virtue – this man is not moved by temptations, as a great rock is not shaken by the wind.

9 If a man puts on the pure yellow robe with a soul which is impure, without self-harmony and truth, he is not worthy of the holy robe.

10 But he who is pure from sin and whose soul is strong in virtue, who has self-harmony and truth, he is worthy of the holy robe.

11 Those who think the unreal is, and think the Real is not, they shall never reach the Truth, lost in the path of wrong thought.

12 But those who know the Real is, and know the unreal is not, they shall indeed reach the Truth, safe on the path of right thought.

13 Even as rain breaks through an ill-thatched house, passions will break through an ill-guarded mind.

14 But even as rain breaks not through a well-thatched house, passions break not through a well-guarded mind.

15 He suffers in this world, and he suffers in the next world: the man who does evil suffers in both worlds. He suffers, he suffers and mourns when he sees the wrong he has done.

16 He is happy in this world and he is happy in the next world: the man who does good is happy in both worlds. He is glad, he feels great gladness when he sees the good he has done.

17 He sorrows in this world, and he sorrows in the next world: the man who does evil sorrows in both worlds. 'I have done evil', thus he laments, and more he laments on the path of sorrow.

18 He rejoices in this world, and he rejoices in the next world: the man who does good rejoices in both worlds. 'I have done good', thus he rejoices, and more he rejoices on the path of joy.

19 If a man speaks many holy words but he speaks and does not, this thoughtless man cannot enjoy the life of holiness: he is like a cowherd who counts the cows of his master.

20 Whereas if a man speaks but a few holy words and yet he lives the life of those words, free from passion and hate and illusion – with right vision and a mind free, craving for nothing both now and hereafter – the life of this man is a life of holiness.

2

WATCHFULNESS

21 Watchfulness is the path of immortality: unwatchfulness is the path of death. Those who are watchful never die: those who do not watch are already as dead.

22 Those who with a clear mind have seen this truth, those who are wise and ever-watchful, they feel the joy of watchfulness, the joy of the path of the Great.

23 And those who in high thought and in deep contemplation with ever-living power advance on the path, they in the end reach NIRVANA, the peace supreme and infinite joy.

24 The man who arises in faith, who ever remembers his high purpose, whose work is pure, and who carefully considers his work, who in self-possession lives the life of perfection, and who ever, for ever, is watchful, that man shall arise in glory.

25 By arising in faith and watchfulness, by self-possession and self-harmony, the wise man makes an island for his soul which many waters cannot overflow.

26 Men who are foolish and ignorant are careless and never watchful; but the man who lives in watchfulness considers it his greatest treasure.

27 Never surrender to carelessness; never sink into weak pleasures and lust. Those who are watchful, in deep contemplation, reach in the end the joy supreme.

28 The wise man who by watchfulness conquers thoughtlessness is as one who free from sorrows ascends the

palace of wisdom and there, from its high terrace, sees those in sorrow below; even as a wise strong man on the holy mountain might behold the many unwise far down below on the plain.

29 Watchful amongst the unwatchful, awake amongst those who sleep, the wise man like a swift horse runs his race, outrunning those who are slow.

30 It was by watchfulness that Indra became the chief of the gods, and thus the gods praise the watchful, and thoughtlessness is ever despised.

31 The monk who has the joy of watchfulness and who looks with fear on thoughtlessness, he goes on his path like a fire, burning all obstacles both great and small.

32 The monk who has the joy of watchfulness, and who looks with fear on thoughtlessness, he can never be deprived of his victory and he is near NIRVANA.

3

THE MIND

33 The mind is wavering and restless, difficult to guard and restrain: let the wise man straighten his mind as a maker of arrows makes his arrows straight.

34 Like a fish which is thrown on dry land, taken from his home in the waters, the mind strives and struggles to get free from the power of Death.

35 The mind is fickle and flighty, it flies after fancies wherever it likes: it is difficult indeed to restrain. But it is a great good to control the mind; a mind self-controlled is a source of great joy.

36 Invisible and subtle is the mind, and it flies after fancies wherever it likes; but let the wise man guard well his mind, for a mind well guarded is a source of great joy.

37 Hidden in the mystery of consciousness, the mind, incorporeal, flies alone far away. Those who set their mind in harmony become free from the bonds of death.

38 He whose mind is unsteady, who knows not the path of Truth, whose faith and peace are ever wavering, he shall never reach fullness of wisdom.

39 But he whose mind in calm self-control is free from the lust of desires, who has risen above good and evil, he is awake and has no fear.

40 Considering that this body is frail like a jar, make your mind strong like a fortress and fight the great fight against MARA, all evil temptations. After victory guard well your conquests, and ever for ever watch.

41 For before long, how sad! this body will lifeless lie on the earth, cast aside like a useless log.

42 An enemy can hurt an enemy, and a man who hates can harm another man; but a man's own mind, if wrongly directed, can do him a far greater harm.

43 A father or a mother, or a relative, can indeed do good to a man; but his own right-directed mind can do to him a far greater good.

4

THE FLOWERS OF LIFE

44 Who shall conquer this world and the world of the gods, and also the world of Yama, of death and of pain? Who shall find the DHAMMAPADA, the clear Path of Perfection, even as a man who seeks flowers finds the most beautiful flower?

45 The wise student shall conquer this world, and the world of the gods, and also the world of Yama, of death and of pain. The wise student shall find the DHAMMAPADA, the clear Path of Perfection, even as a man who seeks flowers finds the most beautiful flower:

46 He who knows that this body is the foam of a wave, the shadow of a mirage, he breaks the sharp arrows of MARA, concealed in the flowers of sensuous passions and, unseen by the King of death, he goes on and follows his path.

47 But death carries away the man who gathers the flowers of sensuous passions, even as a torrent of rushing waters overflows a sleeping village, and then runs forward on its way.

48 And death, the end of all, makes an end of the man who, ever thirsty for desires, gathers the flowers of sensuous passions.

49 As the bee takes the essence of a flower and flies away without destroying its beauty and perfume, so let the sage wander in this life.

50 Think not of the faults of others, of what they have

done or not done. Think rather of your own sins, of the things you have done or not done.

51 Just as a flower which seems beautiful and has colour but has no perfume, so are the fruitless words of the man who speaks them but does them not.

52 And just like a beautiful flower which has colour and also has perfume are the beautiful fruitful words of the man who speaks and does what he says.

53 As from a large heap of flowers many garlands and wreaths can be made, so by a mortal in this life there is much good work to be done.

54 The perfume of flowers goes not against the wind, not even the perfume of sandalwood, of rose-bay, or of jasmine; but the perfume of virtue travels against the wind and reaches unto the ends of the world.

55 There is the perfume of sandalwood, of rose-bay, of the blue lotus and jasmine; but far above the perfume of those flowers the perfume of virtue is supreme.

56 Not very far goes the perfume of flowers, even that of rose-bay or of sandalwood; but the perfume of the good reaches heaven, and it is the perfume supreme amongst the gods.

57 The path of those who are rich in virtue, who are ever watchful, whose true light makes them free, cannot be crossed by MARA, by death.

58 Even as on a heap of rubbish thrown away by the side
59 of the road a lotus flower may grow and blossom with its pure perfume giving joy to the soul, in the same way among the blind multitudes shines pure the light of wisdom of the student who follows the Buddha, the ONE who is truly awake.

5

THE FOOL

60 How long is the night to the watchman; how long is the road to the weary; how long is the wandering of lives ending in death for the fool who cannot find the path!

61 If on the great journey of life a man cannot find one who is better or at least as good as himself, let him joyfully travel alone: a fool cannot help him on his journey.

62 'These are my sons. This is my wealth.' In this way the fool troubles himself. He is not even the owner of himself: how much less of his sons and of his wealth!

63 If a fool can see his own folly, he in this at least is wise; but the fool who thinks he is wise, he indeed is the real fool.

64 If during the whole of his life a fool lives with a wise man, he never knows the path of wisdom as the spoon never knows the taste of the soup.

65 But if a man who watches and sees is only a moment with a wise man he soon knows the path of wisdom, as the tongue knows the taste of the soup.

66 A fool who thinks he is wise goes through life with himself as his enemy, and he ever does wrong deeds which in the end bear bitter fruit.

67 For that deed is not well done when being done one has to repent; and when one must reap with tears the bitter fruits of the wrong deed.

68 But the deed is indeed well done when being done one has not to repent; and when one can reap with joy the sweet fruits of the right deed.

69 The wrong action seems sweet to the fool until the reaction comes and brings pain, and the bitter fruits of wrong deeds have then to be eaten by the fool.

70 A fool may fast month after month eating his food with the sharp point of a blade of *kusa* grass, and his worth be not a sixteenth part of that of the wise man whose thoughts feed on truth.

71 A wrong action may not bring its reaction at once, even as fresh milk turns not sour at once: like a smouldering fire concealed under ashes it consumes the wrongdoer, the fool.

72 And if ever to his own harm the fool increases in cleverness, this only destroys his own mind and his fate is worse than before.

73 For he will wish for reputation, for precedence among the monks, for authority in the monasteries and for veneration amongst the people.

74 'Let householders and hermits, both, think it was I who did that work; and let them ever ask me what they should do or not do.' These are the thoughts of the fool, puffed up with desire and pride.

75 But one is the path of earthly wealth, and another is the path of NIRVANA. Let the follower of Buddha think of this and, without striving for reputation, let him ever strive after freedom.

6

THE WISE MAN

76 Look upon the man who tells thee thy faults as if he told thee of a hidden treasure, the wise man who shows thee the dangers of life. Follow that man: he who follows him will see good and not evil.

77 Let him admonish and let him instruct, and let him restrain what is wrong. He will be loved by those who are good and hated by those who are not.

78 Have not for friends those whose soul is ugly; go not with men who have an evil soul. Have for friends those whose soul is beautiful; go with men whose soul is good.

79 He who drinks of the waters of Truth, he rests in joy with mind serene. The wise find their delight in the DHAMMA, in the Truth revealed by the great.

80 Those who make channels for water control the waters; makers of arrows make the arrows straight; carpenters control their timber; and the wise control their own minds.

81 Even as a great rock is not shaken by the wind, the wise man is not shaken by praise or by blame.

82 Even as a lake that is pure and peaceful and deep, so becomes the soul of the wise man when he hears the words of DHAMMA.

83 Good men, at all times, surrender in truth all attachments. The holy spend not idle words on things of desire. When pleasure or pain comes to them, the wise feel above pleasure and pain.

84 He who for himself or others craves not for sons or power or wealth, who puts not his own success before the success of righteousness, he is virtuous, and righteous, and wise.

85 Few cross the river of time and are able to reach NIRVANA. Most of them run up and down only on this side of the river.

86 But those who when they know the law follow the path of the law, they shall reach the other shore and go beyond the realm of death.

87 Leaving behind the path of darkness and following the
88 path of light, let the wise man leave his home life and go into a life of freedom. In solitude that few enjoy, let him find his joy supreme: free from possessions, free from desires, and free from whatever may darken his mind.

89 For he whose mind is well trained in the ways that lead to light, who surrenders the bondage of attachments and finds joy in his freedom from bondage, who free from the darkness of passions shines pure in a radiance of light, even in this mortal life he enjoys the immortal NIRVANA.

7

INFINITE FREEDOM

90 The traveller has reached the end of the journey! In
the freedom of the Infinite he is free from all sorrows,
the fetters that bound him are thrown away, and the
burning fever of life is no more.

91 Those who have high thoughts are ever striving: they
are not happy to remain in the same place. Like swans
that leave their lake and rise into the air, they leave
their home for a higher home.

92 Who can trace the path of those who know the right
food of life and, rejecting over-abundance, soar in the
sky of liberation, the infinite Void without beginning?
Their course is as hard to follow as that of the birds in
the air.

93 Who can trace the invisible path of the man who soars
in the sky of liberation, the infinite Void without
beginning, whose passions are peace, and over whom
pleasures have no power? His path is as difficult to
trace as that of the birds in the air.

94 The man who wisely controls his senses as a good driver
controls his horses, and who is free from lower passions
and pride, is admired even by the gods.

95 He is calm like the earth that endures; he is steady like
a column that is firm; he is pure like a lake that is clear;
he is free from *Samsara*, the ever-returning life-in-death.

96 In the light of his vision he has found his freedom:
his thoughts are peace, his words are peace and his work
is peace.

97 And he who is free from credulous beliefs since he has seen the eternal NIRVANA, who has thrown off the bondage of the lower life and, far beyond temptations, has surrendered all his desires, he is indeed great amongst men.

98 Wherever holy men dwell, that is indeed a place of joy – be it in the village, or in a forest, or in a valley or on the hills.

99 They make delightful the forests where other people could not dwell. Because they have not the burden of desires, they have that joy which others find not.

8

BETTER THAN A THOUSAND

100 Better than a thousand useless words is one single word that gives peace.

101 Better than a thousand useless verses is one single verse that gives peace.

102 Better than a hundred useless poems is one single poem that gives peace.

103 If a man should conquer in battle a thousand and a
104 thousand more, and another man should conquer him-
105 self, his would be the greater victory, because the greatest of victories is the victory over oneself; and neither the gods in heaven above nor the demons down below can turn into defeat the victory of such a man.

106 If month after month with a thousand offerings for a hundred years one should sacrifice; and another only for a moment paid reverence to a self-conquering man, this moment would have greater value than a hundred years of offerings.

107 If a man for a hundred years should worship the sacred fire in the forest; and if another only for a moment paid reverence to a self-conquering man, this reverence alone would be greater than a hundred years of worship.

108 Whatever a man for a year may offer in worship or in gifts to earn merit is not worth a fraction of the merit earned by one's reverence to a righteous man.

109 And whosoever honours in reverence those who are old in virtue and holiness, he indeed conquers four treasures: long life, and health, and power and joy.

110 Better than a hundred years lived in vice, without contemplation, is one single day of life lived in virtue and in deep contemplation.

111 Better than a hundred years lived in ignorance, without contemplation, is one single day of life lived in wisdom and in deep contemplation.

112 Better than a hundred years lived in idleness and in weakness is a single day of life lived with courage and powerful striving.

113 Better than a hundred years not considering how all things arise and pass away is one single day of life if one considers how all things arise and pass away.

114 Better than a hundred years not seeing one's own immortality is one single day of life if one sees one's own immortality.

115 Better than a hundred years not seeing the Path supreme is one single day of life if one sees the Path supreme.

9

GOOD AND EVIL

116 Make haste and do what is good; keep your mind away from evil. If a man is slow in doing good, his mind finds pleasure in evil.

117 If a man does something wrong, let him not do it again and again. Let him not find pleasure in his sin. Painful is the accumulation of wrongdoings.

118 If a man does something good, let him do it again and again. Let him find joy in his good work. Joyful is the accumulation of good work.

119 A man may find pleasure in evil as long as his evil has not given fruit; but when the fruit of evil comes then that man finds evil indeed.

120 A man may find pain in doing good as long as his good has not given fruit; but when the fruit of good comes then that man finds good indeed.

121 Hold not a sin of little worth, thinking 'this is little to me'. The falling of drops of water will in time fill a water-jar. Even so the foolish man becomes full of evil, although he gather it little by little.

122 Hold not a deed of little worth, thinking 'this is little to me'. The falling of drops of water will in time fill a water-jar. Even so the wise man becomes full of good, although he gather it little by little.

123 Let a man avoid the dangers of evil even as a merchant carrying much wealth, but with a small escort, avoids the dangers of the road, or as a man who loves his life avoids the drinking of poison.

124 As a man who has no wound on his hand cannot be hurt by the poison he may carry in his hand, since poison hurts not where there is no wound, the man who has no evil cannot be hurt by evil.

125 The fool who does evil to a man who is good, to a man who is pure and free from sin, the evil returns to him like the dust thrown against the wind.

126 Some people are born on this earth; those who do evil are reborn in hell; the righteous go to heaven; but those who are pure reach NIRVANA.

127 Neither in the sky, nor deep in the ocean, nor in a mountain-cave, nor anywhere, can a man be free from the evil he has done.

128 Neither in the sky, nor deep in the ocean, nor in a mountain-cave, nor anywhere, can a man be free from the power of death.

10

LIFE

129 All beings tremble before danger, all fear death. When a man considers this, he does not kill or cause to kill.

130 All beings fear before danger, life is dear to all. When a man considers this, he does not kill or cause to kill.

131 He who for the sake of happiness hurts others who also want happiness, shall not hereafter find happiness.

132 He who for the sake of happiness does not hurt others who also want happiness, shall hereafter find happiness.

133 Never speak harsh words, for once spoken they may return to you. Angry words are painful and there may be blows for blows.

134 If you can be in silent quietness like a broken gong that is silent, you have reached the peace of NIRVANA and your anger is peace.

135 Just as a keeper of cows drives his cows into the fields, old age and death drive living beings far into the fields of death.

136 When a fool does evil work, he forgets that he is lighting a fire wherein he must burn one day.

137-140 He who hurts with his weapons those who are harmless and pure shall soon fall into one of these ten evils: fearful pain or infirmity; loss of limbs or terrible disease; or even madness, the loss of the mind; the king's persecution; a fearful indictment; the loss of possessions or the loss of relations; or fire from heaven that may

burn his house. And when the evil-doer is no more, then
he is reborn in hell.

141 Neither nakedness, nor entangled hair, nor uncleanli-
ness, nor fasting, nor sleeping on the ground, nor
covering the body with ashes, nor ever-squatting, can
purify a man who is not pure from doubts and desires.

142 But although a man may wear fine clothing, if he lives
peacefully; and is good, self-possessed, has faith and is
pure; and if he does not hurt any living being, he is a
holy Brahmin, a hermit of seclusion, a monk called a
Bhikkhu.

143 Is there in this world a man so noble that he ever avoids
all blame, even as a noble horse avoids the touch of the
whip?

144 Have fire like a noble horse touched by the whip. By
faith, by virtue and energy, by deep contemplation and
vision, by wisdom and by right action, you shall overcome the sorrows of life.

145 Those who make channels for water control the waters;
makers of arrows make the arrows straight; carpenters
control their timber; and the holy control their soul.

11

BEYOND LIFE

146 How can there be laughter, how can there be pleasure, when the whole world is burning? When you are in deep darkness, will you not ask for a lamp?

147 Consider this body! A painted puppet with jointed limbs, sometimes suffering and covered with ulcers, full of imaginings, never permanent, for ever changing.

148 This body is decaying! A nest of diseases, a heap of corruption, bound to destruction, to dissolution. All life ends in death.

149 Look at these grey-white dried bones, like dried empty gourds thrown away at the end of the summer. Who will feel joy in looking at them?

150 A house of bones is this body, bones covered with flesh and with blood. Pride and hypocrisy dwell in this house and also old age and death.

151 The glorious chariots of kings wear out, and the body wears out and grows old; but the virtue of the good never grows old, and thus they can teach the good to those who are good.

152 If a man tries not to learn he grows old just like an ox! His body indeed grows old but his wisdom does not grow.

153 I have gone round in vain the cycles of many lives ever
154 striving to find the builder of the house of life and death. How great is the sorrow of life that must die! But now I have seen thee, housebuilder: never more

shalt thou build this house. The rafters of sins are broken, the ridge-pole of ignorance is destroyed. The fever of craving is past: for my mortal mind is gone to the joy of the immortal NIRVANA.

155 Those who in their youth did not live in self-harmony, and who did not gain the true treasures of life, are later like long-legged old herons standing sad by a lake without fish.

156 Those who in their youth did not live in self-harmony, and who did not gain the true treasures of life, are later like broken bows, ever deploring old things past and gone.

12

SELF-POSSESSION

157 If a man holds himself dear, let him guard himself well. Of the three watches of his time, let him at least watch over one.

158 Let him find first what is right and then he can teach it to others, avoiding thus useless pain.

159 If he makes himself as good as he tells others to be, then he in truth can teach others. Difficult indeed is self-control.

160 Only a man himself can be the master of himself: who else from outside could be his master? When the Master and servant are one, then there is true help and self-possession.

161 Any wrong or evil a man does, is born in himself and is caused by himself; and this crushes the foolish man as a hard stone grinds the weaker stone.

162 And the evil that grows in a man is like the *malava* creeper which entangles the *sala* tree; and the man is brought down to that condition in which his own enemy would wish him to be.

163 It is easy to do what is wrong, to do what is bad for oneself; but very difficult to do what is right, to do what is good for oneself.

164 The fool who because of his views scorns the teachings of the holy, those whose soul is great and righteous, gathers fruits for his destruction, like the *kashta* reed whose fruits mean its death.

165 By oneself the evil is done, and it is oneself who suffers: by oneself the evil is not done, and by one's Self one becomes pure. The pure and the impure come from oneself: no man can purify another.

166 Let no man endanger his duty, the good of his soul, for the good of another, however great. When he has seen the good of his soul, let him follow it with earnestness.

13

ARISE! WATCH

167 Live not a low life; remember and forget not; follow not wrong ideas; sink not into the world.

168 Arise! Watch. Walk on the right path. He who follows the right path has joy in this world and in the world beyond.

169 Follow the right path: follow not the wrong path. He who follows the right path has joy in this world and in the world beyond.

170 When a man considers this world as a bubble of froth, and as the illusion of an appearance, then the king of death has no power over him.

171 Come and look at this world. It is like a royal painted chariot wherein fools sink. The wise are not imprisoned in the chariot.

172 He who in early days was unwise but later found wisdom, he sheds a light over the world like that of the moon when free from clouds.

173 He who overcomes the evil he has done with the good he afterwards does, he sheds a light over the world like that of the moon when free from clouds.

174 This world is indeed in darkness, and how few can see the light! Just as few birds can escape from a net, few souls can fly into the freedom of heaven.

175 Swans follow the path of the sun by the miracle of flying through the air. Men who are strong conquer evil and its armies; and then they arise far above the world.

176 A man whose words are lies, who transgresses the Great Law, and who scorns the higher world – there is no evil this man may not do.

177 Misers certainly do not go to the heaven of the gods, and fools do not praise liberality; but noble men find joy in generosity, and this gives them joy in higher worlds.

178 Better than power over all the earth, better than going to heaven and better than dominion over the worlds is the joy of the man who enters the river of life that leads to NIRVANA.

14

THE BUDDHA

179 By what earthly path could you entice the Buddha who, enjoying all, can wander through the pathless ways of the Infinite? – the Buddha who is awake, whose victory cannot be turned into defeat, and whom no one can conquer?

180 By what earthly path could you entice the Buddha who, enjoying all, can wander through the pathless ways of the Infinite? – the Buddha who is awake, whom the net of poisonous desire cannot allure?

181 Even the gods long to be like the Buddhas who are awake and watch, who find peace in contemplation and who, calm and steady, find joy in renunciation.

182 It is a great event to be born a man; and his life is an ever-striving. It is not often he hears the doctrine of Truth; and a rare event is the arising of a Buddha.

183 Do not what is evil. Do what is good. Keep your mind pure. This is the teaching of Buddha.

184 Forbearance is the highest sacrifice. NIRVANA is the highest good. This say the Buddhas who are awake. If a man hurts another, he is not a hermit; if he offends another, he is not an ascetic.

185 Not to hurt by deeds or words, self-control as taught in the Rules, moderation in food, the solitude of one's room and one's bed, and the practice of the highest consciousness: this is teaching of the Buddhas who are awake.

186 Since a shower of golden coins could not satisfy craving
187 desires and the end of all pleasure is pain, how could a
wise man find satisfaction even in the pleasures of the
gods? When desires go, joy comes: the follower of
Buddha finds this truth.

188 Men in their fear fly for refuge to mountains or forests,
189 groves, sacred trees or shrines. But those are not a safe
refuge, they are not the refuge that frees a man from
sorrow.

190 He who goes for refuge to Buddha, to Truth and to those
whom he taught, he goes indeed to a great refuge. Then
he sees the four great truths :

191 Sorrow, the cause of sorrow, the end of sorrow, and the
path of eight stages which leads to the end of sorrow.

192 That is the safe refuge, that is the refuge supreme. If a
man goes to that refuge, he is free from sorrow.

193 A man of true vision is not easy to find, a Buddha who is
awake is not born everywhere. Happy are the people
where such a man is born.

194 Happy is the birth of a Buddha, happy is the teaching of
DHAMMA, happy is the harmony of his followers, happy
is the life of those who live in harmony.

195 Who could measure the excellence of the man who
196 pays reverence to those worthy of reverence, a Buddha
or his disciples, who have left evil behind and have
crossed the river of sorrow, who, free from all fear, are
in the glory of NIRVANA?.

15

JOY

197 O let us live in joy, in love amongst those who hate! Among men who hate, let us live in love.

198 O let us live in joy, in health amongst those who are ill! Among men who are ill, let us live in health.

199 O let us live in joy, in peace amongst those who struggle! Among men who struggle, let us live in peace.

200 O let us live in joy, although having nothing! In joy let us live like spirits of light!

201 Victory brings hate, because the defeated man is unhappy. He who surrenders victory and defeat, this man finds joy.

202 There is no fire like lust. There is no evil like hate. There is no pain like disharmony. There is no joy like NIRVANA.

203 The hunger of passions is the greatest disease. Disharmony is the greatest sorrow. When you know this well, then you know that NIRVANA is the greatest joy.

204 Health is the greatest possession. Contentment is the greatest treasure. Confidence is the greatest friend. NIRVANA is the greatest joy.

205 When a man knows the solitude of silence, and feels the joy of quietness, he is then free from fear and sin and he feels the joy of the DHAMMA.

206 It is a joy to see the noble and good, and to be with them makes one happy. If one were able never to see fools, then one could be for ever happy!

207 He who has to walk with fools has a long journey of
sorrow, because to be with a fool is as painful as to be
with an enemy; but the joy of being with the wise is
like the joy of meeting a beloved kinsman.

208 If you find a man who is constant, awake to the inner
light, learned, long-suffering, endowed with devotion, a
noble man – follow this good and great man even as the
moon follows the path of the stars.

16

TRANSIENT PLEASURES

209 He who does what should not be done and fails to do what should be done, who forgets the true aim of life and sinks into transient pleasures – he will one day envy the man who lives in high contemplation.

210 Let a man be free from pleasure and let a man be free from pain; for not to have pleasure is sorrow and to have pain is also sorrow.

211 Be therefore not bound to pleasure for the loss of pleasure is pain. There are no fetters for the man who is beyond pleasure and pain.

212 From pleasure arises sorrow and from pleasure arises fear. If a man is free from pleasure, he is free from fear and sorrow.

213 From passion arises sorrow and from passion arises fear. If a man is free from passion, he is free from fear and sorrow.

214 From sensuousness arises sorrow and from sensuousness arises fear. If a man is free from sensuousness, he is free from fear and sorrow.

215 From lust arises sorrow and from lust arises fear. If a man is free from lust, he is free from fear and sorrow.

216 From craving arises sorrow and from craving arises fear. If a man is free from craving, he is free from fear and sorrow.

217 He who has virtue and vision, who follows DHAMMA,

the Path of Perfection, whose words are truth, and does the work to be done – the world loves such a man.

218 And the man whose mind, filled with determination, is longing for the infinite NIRVANA, and who is free from sensuous pleasures, is called *uddham-soto*, 'he who goes upstream', for against the current of passions and worldly life he is bound for the joy of the Infinite.

219 Just as a man who has long been far away is welcomed
220 with joy on his safe return by his relatives, well-wishers and friends; in the same way the good works of a man in his life welcome him in another life, with the joy of a friend meeting a friend on his return.

17

FORSAKE ANGER

221 Forsake anger, give up pride. Sorrow cannot touch the man who is not in the bondage of anything, who owns nothing.

222 He who can control his rising anger as a coachman controls his carriage at full speed, this man I call a good driver: others merely hold the reins.

223 Overcome anger by peacefulness: overcome evil by good. Overcome the mean by generosity; and the man who lies by truth.

224 Speak the truth, yield not to anger, give what you can to him who asks: these three steps lead you to the gods.

225 The wise who hurt no living being, and who keep their body under self-control, they go to the immortal NIRVANA, where once gone they sorrow no more.

226 Those who are for ever watchful, who study themselves day and night, and who wholly strive for NIRVANA, all their passions pass away.

227 This is an old saying, Atula, it is not a saying of today: 'They blame the man who is silent, they blame the man who speaks too much, and they blame the man who speaks too little'. No man can escape blame in this world.

228 There never was, there never will be, nor is there now, a man whom men always blame, or a man whom they always praise.

229 But who would dare to blame the man whom the wise

230 praise day after day, whose life is pure and full of light, in whom there is virtue and wisdom, who is pure as a pure coin of gold of the Jambu river? Even the gods praise that man, even Brahma the Creator praises him.

231 Watch for anger of the body: let the body be self-controlled. Hurt not with the body, but use your body well.

232 Watch for anger of words: let your words be self-controlled. Hurt not with words, but use your words well.

233 Watch for anger of the mind: let your mind be self-controlled. Hurt not with the mind, but use your mind well.

234 There are men steady and wise whose body, words and mind are self-controlled. They are the men of supreme self-control.

18

HASTEN AND STRIVE

235 Yellow leaves hang on your tree of life. The messengers of death are waiting. You are going to travel far away. Have you any provision for the journey?

236 Make an island for yourself. Hasten and strive. Be wise. With the dust of impurities blown off, and free from sinful passions, you will come unto the glorious land of the great.

237 You are at the end of your life. You are going to meet Death. There is no resting-place on your way, and you have no provision for the journey.

238 Make therefore an island for yourself. Hasten and strive. Be wise. With the dust of impurities blown off, and free from sinful passions, you will be free from birth that must die, you will be free from old age that ends in death.

239 Let a wise man remove impurities from himself even as a silversmith removes impurities from the silver: one after one, little by little, again and again.

240 Even as rust on iron destroys in the end the iron, a man's own impure transgressions lead that man to the evil path.

241 Dull repetition is the rust of sacred verses; lack of repair is the rust of houses; want of healthy exercise is the rust of beauty; unwatchfulness is the rust of the watcher.

242 Misconduct is sin in woman; meanness is sin in a bene-

factor; evil actions are indeed sins both in this world and in the next.

243 But the greatest of all sins is indeed the sin of ignorance. Throw this sin away, O man, and become pure from sin.

244 Life seems easy for those who shamelessly are bold and self-assertive, crafty and cunning, sensuously selfish, wanton and impure, arrogant and insulting, rotting with corruption.

245 But life seems difficult for those who peacefully strive for perfection, who free from self-seeking are not self-assertive, whose life is pure, who see the light.

246 He who destroys life, who utters lies, who takes what
247 is not given to him, who goes to the wife of another, who gets drunk with strong drinks – he digs up the very roots of his life.

248 Know this therefore, O man: that lack of self-control means wrongdoing. Watch that greediness and vice bring thee not unto long suffering.

249 People in this world give their gifts because of inner light or selfish pleasure. If a man's thoughts are disturbed by what others give or give not, how can he by day or night achieve supreme contemplation?

250 But he in whom the roots of jealousy have been uprooted and burnt away, then he both by day or by night can achieve supreme contemplation.

251 There is no fire like lust, and no chains like those of hate. There is no net like illusion, and no rushing torrent like desire.

252 It is easy to see the faults of others, but difficult to see one's own faults. One shows the faults of others like chaff winnowed in the wind, but one conceals one's own faults as a cunning gambler conceals his dice.

253 If a man sees the sins of others and for ever thinks of

their faults, his own sins increase for ever and far off is he from the end of his faults.

254 There is no path in the sky and a monk must find the inner path. The world likes pleasures that are obstacles on the path; but the *Tatha-gatas*, the 'Thus-gone', have crossed the river of time and they have overcome the world.

255 There is no path in the sky and a monk must find the inner path. All things indeed pass away, but the Buddhas are for ever in Eternity.

19

RIGHTEOUSNESS

256 A man is not on the path of righteousness if he settles
257 matters in a violent haste. A wise man calmly considers
what is right and what is wrong, and faces different
opinions with truth, non-violence and peace. This man
is guarded by truth and is a guardian of truth. He is
righteous and he is wise.

258 A man is not called wise because he talks and talks
again; but if he is peaceful, loving and fearless then he
is in truth called wise.

259 A man is not a follower of righteousness because he
talks much learned talk; but although a man be not
learned, if he forgets not the right path, if his work is
rightly done, then he is a follower of righteousness.

260 A man is not old and venerable because grey hairs are
on his head. If a man is old only in years then he is
indeed old in vain.

261 But a man is a venerable 'elder' if he is in truth free
from sin, and if in him there is truth and righteousness,
non-violence, moderation and self-control.

262 Not by mere fine words and appearance can a man be
263 a man of honour, if envy, greed and deceit are in him.
But he in whom these three sins are uprooted and who
is wise and has love, he is in truth a man of honour.

264 Not by the tonsure, a shaven head, does a man become
a *samana*, a monk. How can a man be a *samana* if he
forgets his religious vows, if he speaks what is not true,
if he still has desire and greed?

265 But he who turns into peace all evil, whether this be great or small, he in truth is a *samana*, because all his evil is peace.

266 He is not called a mendicant Bhikkhu because he leads a mendicant life. A man cannot be a true Bhikkhu unless he accepts the law of righteousness and rejects the law of the flesh.

267 But he who is above good and evil, who lives in chastity and goes through life in meditation, he in truth is called a Bhikkhu.

268 If a man is only silent because he is ignorant or a fool,
269 he is not a silent thinker, a MUNI who considers and thinks. But as one who taking a pair of scales, puts in what is good and rejects what is bad, if a man considers the two worlds, then he is called a MUNI of silence, a man who considers and thinks.

270 A man is not a great man because he is a warrior and kills other men; but because he hurts not any living being he in truth is called a great man.

271 Not by mere morals or rituals, by much learning or
272 high concentration, or by a bed of solitude, can I reach that joy of freedom which is not reached by those of the world. Mendicant! Have not self-satisfaction, the victory has not yet been won.

20

THE PATH

273 The best of the paths is the path of eight. The best of truths, the four sayings. The best of states, freedom from passions. The best of men, the one who sees.

274 This is the path. There is no other that leads to vision. Go on this path, and you will confuse MARA, the devil of confusion.

275 Whoever goes on this path travels to the end of his sorrow. I showed this path to the world when I found the roots of sorrow.

276 It is you who must make the effort. The Great of the past only show the way. Those who think and follow the path become free from the bondage of MARA.

277 'All is transient.' When one sees this, he is above sorrow. This is the clear path.

278 'All is sorrow.' When one sees this, he is above sorrow. This is the clear path.

279 'All is unreal.' When one sees this, he is above sorrow. This is the clear path.

280 If a man when young and strong does not arise and strive when he should arise and strive, and thus sinks into laziness and lack of determination, he will never find the path of wisdom.

281 A man should control his words and mind and should not do any harm with his body. If these ways of action are pure he can make progress on the path of the wise.

282 Spiritual Yoga leads to light: lack of Yoga to darkness.

Considering the two paths, let the wise man walk on the path that leads to light.

283 Cut down the forest of desires, not only a tree; for danger is in the forest. If you cut down the forest and its undergrowth, then, Bhikkhus, you will be free on the path of freedom.

284 As long as lustful desire, however small, of man for women is not controlled, so long the mind of man is not free, but is bound like a calf tied to a cow.

285 Pluck out your self-love as you would pull off a faded lotus in autumn. Strive on the path of peace, the path of NIRVANA shown by Buddha.

286 'Here shall I dwell in the season of rains, and here in winter and summer'; thus thinks the fool, but he does not think of death.

287 For death carries away the man whose mind is self-satisfied with his children and his flocks, even as a torrent carries away a sleeping village.

288 Neither father, sons nor one's relations can stop the King of Death. When he comes with all his power, a man's relations cannot save him.

289 A man who is virtuous and wise understands the meaning of this, and swiftly strives with all his might to clear a path to NIRVANA.

21

WAKEFULNESS

290 If by forsaking a small pleasure one finds a great joy, he who is wise will look to the greater and leave what is less.

291 He who seeks happiness for himself by making others unhappy is bound in the chains of hate and from those he cannot be free.

292 By not doing what should be done, and by doing what should not be done, the sinful desires of proud and thoughtless men increase.

293 But those who are ever careful of their actions, who do not what should not be done, are those who are watchful and wise, and their sinful desires come to an end.

294 And a saint, a Brahmin, is pure from past sins; even if he had killed his father and mother, had murdered two noble kings, and had ravaged a whole kingdom and its people.

295 A saint, a Brahmin, is pure from past sins; even if he had killed his father and mother, had murdered two holy kings, and had also murdered the best of men.

296 The followers of Buddha Gotama are awake and for ever watch; and ever by night and by day they remember Buddha, their Master.

297 The followers of Buddha Gotama are awake and for ever watch; and ever by night and by day they remember the Truth of the Law.

298 The followers of Buddha Gotama are awake and for

ever watch; and ever by night and by day they remember the holy brotherhood.

299 The followers of Buddha Gotama are awake and for ever watch; and ever by night and by day they remember the mystery of the body.

300 The followers of Buddha Gotama are awake and for ever watch; and ever by night and by day they find joy in love for all beings.

301 The followers of Buddha Gotama are awake and for ever watch; and ever by night and by day they find joy in supreme contemplation.

302 It is painful to leave the world; it is painful to be in the world; and it is painful to be alone amongst the many. The long road of transmigration is a road of pain for the traveller: let him rest by the road and be free.

303 If a man has faith and has virtue, then he has true glory and treasure. Wherever that man may go, there he will be held in honour.

304 The good shine from far away, like the Himalaya mountains; but the wicked are in darkness, like arrows thrown in the night.

305 He who can be alone and rest alone and is never weary of his great work, he can live in joy, when master of himself, by the edge of the forest of desires.

22

IN DARKNESS

306 He who says what is not goes down the path of hell; and he who says he has not done what he knows well he has done. Both in the end have to suffer, because both sinned against truth.

307 Many wear the yellow robe whose life is not pure, who have not self-control. Those evil men through their evil deeds are reborn in a hell of evil.

308 For it were better for an evil man to swallow a ball of red-hot iron rather than he should eat offerings of food given to him by good people.

309 Four things happen to the thoughtless man who takes another man's wife: he lowers himself, his pleasure is restless, he is blamed by others, he goes to hell.

310 Yes. The degradation of the soul, a frightened pleasure, the danger of the law, the path of hell. Considering these four, let not a man go after another man's wife.

311 Just as a hand of *kusa* grass if badly grasped will cut one's hand, the life of a monk, if imperfectly followed, will only lead him to hell.

312 For when acts of devotion are carelessly performed, when sacred vows are broken, and when the holy life is not pure, no great fruit can come from such a life.

313 When a man has something to do, let him do it with all his might. A thoughtless pilgrim only raises dust on the road – the dust of dangerous desires.

314 Better to do nothing than to do what is wrong, for

wrongdoing brings burning sorrow. Do therefore what is right, for good deeds never bring pain.

315 Like a border town that is well guarded both within and without, so let a man guard himself, and let not a moment pass by in carelessness. Those who carelessly allow their life to pass by, in the end have to suffer in hell.

316 Those who are ashamed when they should not be ashamed, and who are not ashamed when they should be, are men of very wrong views and they go the downward path.

317 Those who fear what they should not fear, and who do not fear what they should fear, are men of very wrong views and they go the downward path.

318 Those who think that right is wrong, and who think that wrong is right, they are the men of wrong views and they go the downward path.

319 But those who think that wrong is wrong, and who think that right is right, they are the men of right views and they go on the upward path.

23

ENDURANCE

320 I will endure words that hurt in silent peace as the strong elephant endures in battle arrows sent by the bow, for many people lack self-control.

321 They take trained elephants to battle, and kings ride on royal trained elephants. The best of men are self-trained men, those who can endure abuse in peace.

322 Mules when trained are good, and so are noble horses of Sindh. Strong elephants when trained are good; but the best is the man who trains himself.

323 For it is not with those riding animals that a man will reach the land unknown. NIRVANA is reached by that man who wisely, heroically, trains himself.

324 The great elephant called Dhana-palaka is hard to control when in rut, and he will not eat his food when captive, for he remembers the elephant grove.

325 The man who is lazy and a glutton, who eats large meals and rolls in sleep, who is like a pig which is fed in the sty, this fool is reborn to a life of death.

326 In days gone by this mind of mine used to stray wherever selfish desire or lust or pleasure would lead it. To-day this mind does not stray and is under the harmony of control, even as a wild elephant is controlled by the trainer.

327 Find joy in watchfulness; guard well your mind. Uplift yourself from your lower self, even as an elephant draws himself out of a muddy swamp.

328 If on the journey of life a man can find a wise and intelligent friend who is good and self-controlled, let him go with that traveller; and in joy and recollection let them overcome the dangers of the journey.

329 But if on the journey of life a man cannot find a wise and intelligent friend who is good and self-controlled, let him then travel alone, like a king who has left his country, or like a great elephant alone in the forest.

330 For it is better to go alone on the path of life rather than to have a fool for a companion. With few wishes and few cares, and leaving all sins behind, let a man travel alone, like a great elephant alone in the forest.

331 It is sweet to have friends in need; and to share enjoyment is sweet. It is sweet to have done good before death; and to surrender all pain is sweet.

332 It is sweet in this world to be a mother; and to be a father is sweet. It is sweet in this world to be a monk; and to be a saintly Brahmin is sweet.

333 It is sweet to enjoy a lifelong virtue; and a pure firm faith is sweet. It is sweet to attain wisdom; and to be free from sin is sweet.

24

CRAVINGS

334 If a man watches not for NIRVANA, his cravings grow like a creeper and he jumps from death to death like a monkey in the forest from one tree without fruit to another.

335 And when his cravings overcome him, his sorrows increase more and more, like the entangling creeper called *birana*.

336 But whoever in this world overcomes his selfish cravings, his sorrows fall away from him, like drops of water from a lotus flower.

337 Therefore in love I tell you, to you all who have come here: Cut off the bonds of desires, as the surface grass creeper *birana* is cut for its fragant root called *usira*. Be not like a reed by a stream which MARA, the devil of temptation, crushes again and again.

338 Just as a tree, though cut down, can grow again and again if its roots are undamaged and strong, in the same way if the roots of craving are not wholly uprooted sorrows will come again and again.

339 When the thirty-six streams of desire that run towards pleasures are strong, their powerful waves carry away that man without vision whose imaginings are lustful desires.

340 Everywhere flow the streams. The creeper of craving grows everywhere. If you see the creeper grow, cut off its roots by the power of wisdom.

341 The sensuous pleasures of men flow everywhere. Bound for pleasures and seeking pleasures men suffer life and old age.

342 Men who are pursued by lust run around like a hunted hare. Held in fetters and in bonds they suffer and suffer again.

343 Men who are pursued by lust run round like a hunted hare. For a monk to conquer lust he must first conquer desires.

344 The man who free from desires finds joy in solitude, but when free he then returns to his life of old desires, people can say of that man: 'He was free and he ran back to his prison!'

345 The wise do not call a strong fetter that which is made of iron, of wood or of rope; much stronger is the fetter of passion for gold and for jewels, for sons or for wives.

346 This is indeed a strong fetter, say the wise. It seems soft but it drags a man down, and it is hard to undo. Therefore some men cut their fetters, renounce the life of the world and start to walk on the path, leaving pleasures behind.

347 Those who are slaves of desires run into the stream of desires, even as a spider runs into the web that it made. Therefore some men cut their fetters and start to walk on the path, leaving sorrows behind.

348 Leave the past behind; leave the future behind; leave the present behind. Thou art then ready to go to the other shore. Never more shalt thou return to a life that ends in death.

349 The man who is disturbed by wrong thoughts, whose selfish passions are strong and who only seeks sensuous pleasures, increases his craving desires and makes stronger the chains he forges for himself.

350 But he who enjoys peaceful thoughts, who considers the

sorrows of pleasure, and who ever remembers the light
of his life – he will see the end of his cravings, he will
break the chains of death.

351 He has reached the end of his journey, he trembles not,
his cravings are gone, he is free from sin, he has burnt
the thorns of life : this is his last mortal body.

352 He is free from lust, he is free from greed, he knows
the meaning of words, and the meaning of their com-
binations, he is a great man, a great man who sees the
Light : this is his last mortal body.

353 I have conquered all; I know all, and my life is pure;
I have left all, and I am free from craving. I myself
found the way. Whom shall I call Teacher? Whom shall
I teach?

354 The gift of Truth conquers all gifts. The taste of Truth
conquers all sweetness. The Joy of Truth conquers all
pleasures. The loss of desires conquers all sorrows.

355 Wealth destroys the fool who seeks not the Beyond.
Because of greed for wealth the fool destroys himself as
if he were his own enemy.

356 Weeds harm the fields, passions harm human nature :
offerings given to those free from passions bring a
great reward.

357 Weeds harm the fields, hate harms human nature :
offerings given to those free from hate bring a great
reward.

358 Weeds harm the fields, illusion harms human nature :
offerings given to those free from illusion bring a great
reward.

359 Weeds harm the fields, desire harms human nature :
offerings given to those free from desire bring a great
reward.

25

THE MONK

360 Good is the control of the eye, and good is the control of the ear; good is the control of smell, and good is the control of taste.

361 Good is the control of the body, and good is the control of words; good is the control of the mind, and good is the control of our whole inner life. When a monk has achieved perfect self-control, he leaves all sorrows behind.

362 The man whose hands are controlled, whose feet are controlled, whose words are controlled, who is self-controlled in all things, who finds the inner joy, whose mind is self-possessed, who is one and has found perfect peace – this man I call a monk.

363 The monk whose words are controlled, peaceful and wise, who is humble, who throws light on the letter and the spirit of the sacred verses – sweet are his words.

364 Who abides in the truth of DHAMMA, whose joy is in the truth of DHAMMA, who ponders on DHAMMA, and remembers the truth of DHAMMA – this monk shall never fall from DHAMMA, from Truth.

365 Let him not despise the offerings given to him, and let him not be jealous of others, because the monk who feels envy cannot achieve deep contemplation.

366 However little a monk may receive, if he despises not what he receives, even the gods praise that monk, whose life is pure and full of endeavour.

367 For whom 'name and form' are not real, who never feels 'this is mine', and who sorrows not for things that are not, he in truth can be called a monk.

368 The monk who is full of love and who fully lives in the law of Buddha, he follows the path of NIRVANA, the path of the end of all sorrow, the path of infinite joy.

369 Empty the boat of your life, O man; when empty it will swiftly sail. When empty of passions and harmful desires you are bound for the land of NIRVANA.

370 Cut off the five – selfishness, doubt, wrong austerities and rites, lust, hate; throw off the five – desire to be born with a body, or without a body, self-will, restlessness, ignorance; but cherish five – faith, watchfulness, energy, contemplation, vision. He who has broken the five fetters – lust, hate, delusion, pride, false views – is one who has crossed to the other shore.

371 Watch, Bhikkhu. Be in high contemplation, and think not of pleasure, so that you have not to think of pain, like those who in the fire of hell have to swallow a ball of red-hot iron.

372 He who has not wisdom has not contemplation, and he who has not contemplation has not wisdom; but he who has wisdom and contemplation, he is very near NIRVANA.

373 When with a mind in silent peace a monk enters his empty house, then he feels the unearthly joy of beholding the light of Truth.

374 And when he sees in a clear vision the coming and going of inner events, then he feels the infinite joy of those who see the immortal THAT; the NIRVANA immortal.

375 This is the beginning of the life of a wise monk; self-control of the senses, happiness, living under the moral law, and the association with good friends whose life is pure and who are ever striving.

376 Let him live in love. Let his work be well done. Then in a fulness of joy he will see the end of sorrow.

377 Even as the *vasika* jasmine lets its withered flowers fall, do you let fall from you, O monks, all ill passions and all ill-will.

378 The monk is said to be a Bhikkhu of peace when his body, words and mind are peaceful, when he is master of himself and when he has left behind the lower attractions of the world.

379 Arise! Rouse thyself by thy Self; train thyself by thy Self. Under the shelter of thy Self, and ever watchful, thou shalt live in supreme joy.

380 For thy Self is the master of thyself, and thy Self is thy refuge. Train therefore thyself well, even as a merchant trains a fine horse.

381 In a fulness of delight and of faith in the teaching of Buddha, the mendicant monk finds peace supreme and, beyond the transience of time, he will find the joy of Eternity, the joy supreme of NIRVANA.

382 When a mendicant monk, though young, follows with faith the path of Buddha, his light shines bright over the world, like the brightness of a moon free from clouds.

26

THE BRAHMIN

383 Go beyond the stream, Brahmin, go with all your soul: leave desires behind. When you have crossed the stream of *Samsara*, you will reach the land of NIRVANA.

384 When beyond meditation and contemplation a Brahmin has reached the other shore, then he attains the supreme vision and all his fetters are broken.

385 He for whom there is neither this nor the further shore, nor both, who, beyond all fear, is free – him I call a Brahmin.

386 He who lives in contemplation, who is pure and is in peace, who has done what was to be done, who is free from passions, who has reached the Supreme end – him I call a Brahmin.

387 By day the sun shines, and by night shines the moon. The warrior shines in his armour, and the Brahmin priest in his meditation. But the Buddha shines by day and by night – in the brightness of his glory shines the man who is awake.

388 Because he has put away evil, he is called a Brahmin; because he lives in peace, he is called a *Samana*; because he leaves all sins behind, he is called a *Pabbajita*, a pilgrim.

389 One should never hurt a Brahmin; and a Brahmin should never return evil for evil. Alas for the man who hurts a Brahmin! Alas for the Brahmin who returns evil for evil!

390 It is not a little good that a Brahmin gains if he holds back his mind from the pleasures of life. Every time the desire to hurt stops, every time a pain disappears.

391 He who hurts not with his thoughts, or words or deeds, who keeps these three under control – him I call a Brahmin.

392 He who learns the law of righteousness from one who teaches what Buddha taught, let him revere his teacher, as a Brahmin reveres the fire of sacrifice.

393 A man becomes not a Brahmin by long hair or family or birth. The man in whom there is truth and holiness, he is in joy and he is a Brahmin.

394 Of what use is your tangled hair, foolish man, of what use your antelope garment, if within you have tangled cravings, and without ascetic ornaments?

395 The man who is clothed in worn-out garments, thin, whose veins stand out, who in the forest is alone in contemplation – him I call a Brahmin.

396 I call not a man a Brahmin because he was born from a certain family or mother, for he may be proud, and he may be wealthy. The man who is free from possessions and free from desires – him I call a Brahmin.

397 He who has cut all fetters and whose mind trembles not, who in infinite freedom is free from all bonds – him I call a Brahmin.

398 Who has cut off the strap, the thong and the rope, with all their fastenings, who has raised the bar that closes the door, who is awake – him I call a Brahmin.

399 Who, though innocent, suffers insults, stripes and chains, whose weapons are endurance and soul-force – him I call a Brahmin.

400 Who is free from anger, faithful to his vows, virtuous,

free from lusts, self-trained, whose mortal body is his last – him I call a Brahmin.

401 Who clings not to sensuous pleasures, even as water clings not to the leaf of the lotus, or a grain of mustard seed to the point of a needle – him I call a Brahmin.

402 He who even in this life knows the end of sorrow, who has laid down his burden and is free – him I call a Brahmin.

403 He whose vision is deep, who is wise, who knows the path and what is outside the path, who has attained the highest end – him I call a Brahmin.

404 Who keeps away from those who have a home and from those who have not a home, who wanders alone, and who has few desires – him I call a Brahmin.

405 Who hurts not any living being, whether feeble or strong, who neither kills nor causes to kill – him I call a Brahmin.

406 Who is tolerant to the intolerant, peaceful to the violent, free from greed with the greedy – him I call a Brahmin.

407 He from whom lust and hate, and pride and insincerity fall down like a mustard seed from the point of a needle – him I call a Brahmin.

408 He who speaks words that are peaceful and useful and true, words that offend no one – him I call a Brahmin.

409 Who in this world does not take anything not given to him: be it long or short, large or small, good or bad – him I call a Brahmin.

410 He who has no craving desires, either for this world or for another world, who free from desires is in infinite freedom – him I call a Brahmin.

411 He who in his vision is free from doubts and, having all, longs for nothing, for he has reached the immortal NIRVANA – him I call a Brahmin.

412 He who in this world has gone beyond good and evil and both, who free from sorrows is free from passions and is pure – him I call a Brahmin.

413 He who like the moon is pure, bright, clear and serene; whose pleasure for things that pass away is gone – him I call a Brahmin.

414 He who has gone beyond the illusion of *Samsara*, the muddy road of transmigration so difficult to pass; who has crossed to the other shore and, free from doubts and temporal desires, has reached in his deep contemplation the joy of NIRVANA – him I call a Brahmin.

415 He who wanders without a home in this world, leaving behind the desires of the world, and the desires never return – him I call a Brahmin.

416 He who wanders without a home in this world, leaving behind the feverish thirst for the world, and the fever never returns – him I call a Brahmin.

417 He who is free from the bondage of men and also from the bondage of the gods: who is free from all things in creation – him I call a Brahmin.

418 He who is free from pleasure and pain, who is calm, and whose seeds of death-in-life are burnt, whose heroism has conquered all the inner worlds – him I call a Brahmin.

419 He who knows the going and returning of beings – the birth and rebirth of life – and in joy has arrived at the end of his journey, and now he is awake and can see – him I call a Brahmin.

420 He whose path is not known by men, nor by spirits or gods, who is pure from all imperfections, who is a saint, an Arahat – him I call a Brahmin.

421 He for whom things future or past or present are nothing, who has nothing and desires nothing – him I call a Brahmin.

422 He who is powerful, noble, who lives a life of inner heroism, the all-seer, the all-conqueror, the ever-pure, who has reached the end of the journey, who like Buddha is awake – him I call a Brahmin.

423 He who knows the river of his past lives and is free from life that ends in death, who knows the joys of heaven and the sorrows of hell, for he is a seer whose vision is pure, who in perfection is one with the Supreme Perfection – him I call a Brahmin.